A PRIMARY SOURCE HISTORY
OF THE UNITED STATES

AMERICA IN TODAY'S WORLD

1969–2004

George E. Stanley

WORLD ALMANAC® LIBRARY

Please visit our web site at: www.worldalmanaclibrary.com
For a free color catalog describing World Almanac® Library's list of high-quality
books and multimedia programs, call 1-800-848-2928 (USA) or 1-800-387-3178
(Canada). World Almanac® Library's fax: (414) 332-3567.

Library of Congress Cataloging-in-Publication Data available upon request from publisher.
Fax (414) 336-0157 for the attention of the Publishing Records Department.

ISBN 0-8368-5831-X (lib. bdg.)
ISBN 0-8368-5840-9 (softcover)

First published in 2005 by
World Almanac® Library
330 West Olive Street, Suite 100
Milwaukee, WI 53212 USA

Produced by Byron Preiss Visual Publications Inc.
Project Editor: Susan Hoe
Designer: Marisa Gentile
World Almanac® Library editor: Alan Wachtel
World Almanac® Library art direction: Tammy West

Picture acknowledgements:
AP/Wide World Photos: Cover (upper left), pp. 7, 8, 16, 28, 29, 31, 33, 37, 38, 39, 41, 42;
Courtesy of the Ronald Reagan Library: Cover (lower right), pp. 18, 21 (upper right), 21 (lower left),
22; The Granger Collection: Cover (lower left); Library of Congress: Cover (upper right), pp. 4, 9,
12, 13, 15, 24, 26, 32, 36

Printed in the United States of America

1 2 3 4 5 6 7 8 9 09 08 07 06 05

Dr. George E. Stanley is a professor at Cameron University in Lawton, Oklahoma. He has authored
more than eighty books for young readers, many in the field of history and science. Dr. Stanley recently
completed a series of history books on famous Americans, including *Geronimo, Andrew Jackson,
Harry S. Truman*, and *Mr. Rogers*.

CONTENTS

Through the examination of authentic historical documents, including charters, diaries, journals, letters, speeches, and other written records, each title in *A Primary Source History of the United States* offers a unique perspective on the events that shaped the United States. In addition to providing important historical information, each document serves as a piece of living history that opens a window into the kinds of thinking and modes of expression that characterized the various epochs of American history.

Note: To facilitate the reading of older documents, the modern-day spelling of certain words is used.

CHAPTER 1

The Nixon and Ford Years

1969–1976

At the close of the 1960s, the 1968 presidential election was about to take place. The Republicans chose Richard M. Nixon as their candidate. He emphasized law and order and said he had a "secret plan" to end the war in Vietnam. Nixon won the election, but the Democrats retained control of both houses of Congress.

Unlike the two previous presidents, John F. Kennedy and Lyndon B. Johnson, President Richard Nixon did not have a deep commitment to social programs and the civil rights movement. He believed that he had been elected president because of the support he received from what he called the "silent majority"—middle-class Americans who had grown wary of "big" government and its involvement in their lives. With that in mind, Nixon vetoed a number of bills related to health and education. He was also not very interested in enforcing civil rights legislation, particularly those laws that were related to school desegregation.

Nixon tried to address America's economic problems—including the challenge of keeping inflation under control—with a policy he called the "New Federalism," which gave individual

▲ A 1971 photograph of President Richard M. Nixon at his daughter's White House wedding.

states more fiscal responsibility. In 1972, Congress passed revenue sharing legislation, a plan that would allow the federal government to provide grants to cities and states to use as they saw fit instead of having the federal government set the guidelines.

During his administration, Nixon ended the draft, passed new anti-crime laws, and appointed conservative justices to the courts. But his major accomplishments as president were in the field of foreign policy.

NIXON AND THE VIETNAM WAR

President Nixon's plan for ending the war was called Vietnamization. It was based on the premise that the South Vietnamese would gradually take over the fighting, as more and more American troops left the country. In June 1969, while continuing the Paris peace talks, which had been started by President Johnson, Nixon ordered the withdrawal of twenty-five thousand American soldiers. However, at the same time, without telling Congress or the American people, Nixon ordered a secret bombing campaign in neighboring Cambodia to keep the North Vietnamese from crossing into Cambodian territory to take troops and supplies to South Vietnam.

On April 30, 1970, South Vietnamese and American forces invaded Cambodia to search for weapons and enemy forces. It wasn't long, however, before news about the year-old "secret" bombings leaked out, and an outraged U.S. Senate reacted by terminating the 1964 Tonkin Gulf Resolution, which had allowed the president to make war decisions without consulting Congress.

The incursion and the news of the secret bombings of Cambodia also sparked a new wave of antiwar protests—especially on college campuses—around the country. On May 4, 1970, National Guard troops, called in to confront a peaceful protest at Ohio's Kent State University, fired at students, many of whom were not participating in the protest, killing four. Americans were horrified by what they saw. At Jackson State University in Mississippi, two more students were killed during another protest. To many Americans, it seemed as if the government was waging war against its own people.

The antiwar movement continued into 1971. The morale of the American troops was now negatively affected not only by what they saw as unclear military goals but by what was happening in the streets of their hometowns.

NIXON'S ADDRESS ON CAMBODIA: 1970

... Ten days ago ... I announced a decision to withdraw an additional 150,000 Americans from Vietnam over the next year ... despite our concern over increased enemy activity in Laos, in Cambodia, and in South Vietnam....

To protect our men who are in Vietnam and to guarantee the continued success of our withdrawal and Vietnamization programs, I have concluded that the time has come for action....

Tonight American and South Vietnamese units will attack [North Vietnam military sanctuaries in Cambodia]....

The areas [in Cambodia] ... are ... controlled by North Vietnamese forces....

During my campaign for the Presidency, I pledged to bring Americans home from Vietnam. They are coming home.

I promised to end this war. I shall keep that promise.

I promised to win a just peace. I shall keep that promise.

... But we are also determined to put an end to this war....

THE VIETNAM WAR ENDS

By 1972, President Nixon had reduced the number of American troops in Vietnam by half of what it had been, but the bombing raids continued in North Vietnam, Laos, and Cambodia. In January 1973, the South Vietnamese and the North Vietnamese governments signed the Paris Peace Accord, which was subtitled an "Agreement on Ending the War and Restoring Peace in Vietnam." All American troops were withdrawn, and more than five hundred American prisoners of war (POWs) were returned. Now only a few thousand American workers remained in Vietnam, along with a small military staff at the embassy in Saigon.

In March 1975, the North Vietnamese broke the truce and made their final assault on South Vietnam. Millions of refugees fled their homes, desperately trying to reach the coast, so that they could escape by boat, or to reach what they perceived was the safety of Saigon.

On April 30, 1975, as the last helicopters lifted off the roof of the American embassy, the South Vietnamese government surrendered to the North Vietnamese. The long

Vietnam War was over. Communists finally controlled the entire country.

A long period of adjustment followed the end of the Vietnam War. It was especially difficult for returning veterans. Many of them were harassed or blamed for "losing" the war. Prisoners of war were the exception. Many of them received a hero's welcome, because they had survived humiliation and torture for years. Although most veterans resumed normal lives, thousands of others found it difficult to do so. Many veterans suffered from post-traumatic stress disorder, and many had trouble finding jobs. Some fell into drug and alcohol addiction.

▲ Even Vietnam army nurses (like author Van Devanter) encountered difficult homecomings.

Lynda Van Devanter served a year as an army nurse in Vietnam. In 1983, she wrote a highly acclaimed book, *Home Before Morning*, which told about the brutality of the war and of

LYNDA VAN DEVANTER'S *HOME BEFORE MORNING:* 1983

… I checked into commercial buses and taxis, but none were running. There was a transit strike on … [so] I stuck out my thumb and waited. I was no stranger to hitchhiking. It was the only way to get around in Vietnam….

But hitchhiking in the real world … was nowhere near as easy—especially if you were wearing a uniform…. A few drivers … slowed long enough to yell obscenities. One threw a carton of trash and another nearly hit me with a half-empty can of soda…. Finally, two guys stopped….

"Going anywhere near the airport?" I asked.

"Sure am," [one of the guys] said…. "We're going past the airport, sucker, but we don't take Army pigs." He spit on me. I was stunned….

NIXON AND CHINA

In 1969, Soviet and Chinese troops battled each other along their common border. To Americans, it looked as though long-standing disagreements between the two countries were beginning to widen. President Nixon recognized that his previous notion about the Communist world was wrong—that it was no longer just one united group of countries focused on destroying the United States and its allies. Nixon saw an opportunity to play China and the Soviet Union against each other to the advantage of the United States. The president also thought that if he improved America's relations with China, China might then pressure North Vietnam to end the Vietnam War.

In 1971, an American table tennis team visited China and received a very hospitable welcome. This "ping-pong diplomacy," as it was known, paved the way for a secret visit to China in July by Nixon's secretary of state and top foreign policy adviser, Henry Kissinger. Nixon himself visited China in February 1972. Prior to the visit, Kissinger wrote a memo to him, in an effort to prepare the president for diplomacy with the Chinese.

Although formal diplomatic relations were not established until 1979, cultural exchanges began almost immediately. In 1972, Chinese acrobats performed in the United States, and in 1973, the Philadelphia Symphony Orchestra played in China.

▲ President Nixon meeting with Mao Zedong *(center)* and Zhou Enlai *(far left)*.

KISSINGER'S TOP SECRET MEMORANDUM TO PRESIDENT NIXON: 1972

... [The Chinese] are ... realists who calculate they need us because of a threatening Soviet Union, a resurgent Japan, and a potentially independent Taiwan....

The Chinese leaders are deadly serious people who will not be swayed from their convictions....

Chou [Zhou Enlai, former chairman of the Chinese Communist Party] ... ranks with De Gaulle [of France] as the most impressive statesman I have ever met ... [although some diplomats] consider Mao [Zedong, current chairman] even more impressive....

They will make a truly imposing and formidable pair....

NIXON AND THE SOVIET UNION

Just a few months after his visit to China, President Nixon met with Soviet leader Leonid Brezhnev in Moscow to try to find a way to ease the tensions that had existed between the two countries since the end of World War II. The president didn't want what was known as the "Cold War" to turn into a nuclear war. He was able to convince Brezhnev to sign a military agreement called the Strategic Arms Limitation Talks, or SALT I, which called a halt to the building of any new defensive anti-ballistic missiles and offensive intercontinental ballistic missiles on the part of both countries. It was hoped that war would be deterred, since neither the United States nor the Soviet Union would want to trigger its own destruction. Although SALT I did not mean an end to the Cold War, it did forestall a costly new arms race that the United States did not want and that the Soviet Union could not afford.

▲ A 1961 photo of Leonid Brezhnev, (*left*) and then Soviet premiere Nikita Khrushchev (*right*).

THE ABORTION CONTROVERSY

Prior to 1820, the United States had only a few laws against abortion, but the anti-abortion movement had accelerated during the 1860s, and by 1900, abortion was all but illegal.

With the rise of feminism in the 1960s, the issue of abortion came to the forefront. In 1970, Jane Roe (not her real name) challenged Texas's anti-abortion law in court because she said it violated her right to privacy. The Texas court ruled against her, but the decision was appealed all the way to the Supreme Court, which said in *Roe* v. *Wade* in 1973 that a woman had an unlimited right to an abortion in the first trimester but that in the second and third trimesters, states may intervene to save the unborn child, except where the mother's health is at risk.

Many people who were against legal abortion turned to direct confrontations with the women seeking abortions and the doctors and nurses who provided them. They picketed and blocked the entrances to abortion clinics. Some of these confrontations turned violent, and several people were killed.

66 The abortion decision must be left to the medical judgment of the pregnant woman's attending physician. 99

ROE v. *WADE* SUPREME COURT DECISION: 1973

... For the stage prior to approximately the end of the first trimester, the abortion decision ... must be left to the medical judgment of the pregnant woman's attending physician....

For the stage subsequent to viability, the State in promoting its interest in the potentiality of human life may, if it chooses, regulate, even proscribe, abortion except where it is necessary, in appropriate medical judgment, for the preservation of the life or health of the mother....

This holding, we feel, is consistent with the relative weights of the respective interests involved, with the lessons and examples of medical and legal history, with the lenity of the common law, and with the demands of the profound problems of the present day....

WATERGATE

In June 1972, five men were arrested when they attempted to bug the Democratic National Committee headquarters at the Watergate Hotel in Washington, D.C. One of the men was James McCord, a member of President Nixon's campaign staff.

The president was reelected in November, but the Watergate scandal would not go away. The *Washington Post* newspaper reported a connection to the Nixon administration. This prompted the Senate to open hearings on the matter, which exposed presidential abuse of power. When, in August 1974, it became clear to Nixon that he would be impeached, he made the decision to resign.

PRESIDENT NIXON'S RESIGNATION SPEECH: 1974

... In the past few days ... it has become evident to me that I no longer have a strong enough political base ... to justify [staying in office]....

I have never been a quitter ... [but] America needs a full-time President and a full-time Congress....

Therefore, I shall resign the Presidency effective at noon tomorrow....

I regret deeply any injuries that may have been done in the course of the events that led to this decision. I would say only that if some of my judgments were wrong, and some were wrong, they were made in what I believed at the time to be the best interest of the Nation....

GERALD FORD BECOMES PRESIDENT

At Nixon's resignation, Vice President Gerald Ford became president. Hoping to put an end to the Watergate scandal, he gave President Nixon a formal pardon, but most Americans believed he was only doing his old boss a favor.

Unfortunately, President Ford was unable to solve the domestic problems of inflation and high unemployment of the time, but in foreign affairs, he began the SALT II negotiations with the Soviet Union that would further limit missile systems. Most Americans liked President Ford, but they could never quite disassociate him from the Nixon administration.

CHAPTER 2

The Carter Years

1976–1980

In 1976, when former Georgia governor Jimmy Carter was elected president over Gerald Ford, he announced that he was going to use U.S. foreign policy to promote respect for human rights in all dealings with other countries. He sought better relations with the nations of Africa and told the governments of Chile, Nicaragua, South Africa, and South Korea that they had to respect the civil rights of their citizens if they wanted to receive any kind of American aid.

Because Carter believed that the Panama Canal really belonged to Panama and that the United States should not have "perpetual" control of it, he persuaded Congress to give up ownership of not only the canal but the Canal Zone—the land bordering the waterway on both sides—by 1999. The treaty was ratified by the Senate in 1978.

That same year, President Carter announced that the United States would establish full diplomatic relations with Communist China on January 1, 1979, and that diplomatic ties with the Nationalist government of Taiwan, an island off the coast of China, would be severed. Although some people felt that Carter was betraying a long time anti-Communist ally, most Americans believed that U.S. diplomatic recognition of the Communist government of China would help to keep peace between the two countries.

▲ President Jimmy Carter greets Rev. Martin Luther King Sr. in 1976.

ENERGY CRISIS

In 1973, the price of oil skyrocketed when OPEC, the Organization of Petroleum Exporting Countries, stopped shipments to the United States for a few months, causing long lines at gas stations. To guard against another crisis, President Carter created the Department of Energy, which he hoped would address the problem, but in 1979, another global shortage of oil once again caused long lines at the gas pumps. Americans wondered if this recurring energy crisis could ever be permanently solved. With this new shortage coming so soon after the Vietnam War and the Watergate scandal, Americans began

▲ The oil shortage in 1979 created long gas lines.

to see their future as bleak. President Carter believed that this "crisis of confidence" in America's future was the reason the United States was unable to overcome its energy problem. In 1979, instead of giving a speech in which he discussed only the nation's energy crisis, Carter first addressed this more personal issue.

CARTER'S "ENERGY AND NATIONAL GOALS" ADDRESS: 1979

... I want to talk to you ... about a fundamental threat to [our] democracy....

It is a crisis of confidence ... [that] is threatening to destroy the social and the political fabric of America....

We can take the first steps ... to solve our energy problem....

I'm proposing a bold conservation program ... [that asks] every average American ... to build conservation into your homes and your lives....

Every act of energy conservation ... is an act of patriotism....

So, the solution of our energy crisis can also help us to conquer the crisis of the spirit in our country. It can rekindle our sense of unity, our confidence in the future, and give ... all of us individually a new sense of purpose....

For a short time after the speech, President Carter's approval ratings climbed. In response, people turned down their thermostats, car-pooled, and bought more fuel-efficient cars.

CARTER AND THE SOVIET UNION

As it had been with Presidents Nixon and Ford, *détente* with the Soviet Union remained a high priority for President Carter. In June 1979, he and Soviet premier Brezhnev signed the SALT II accord, which had been initiated during President Ford's administration, further reducing the nuclear arsenal of both countries, but the progress of *détente* came to an abrupt halt in December 1979, when the Soviet Union invaded Afghanistan to shore up a faltering Communist government under siege by Muslim rebels.

As a protest, Carter withdrew SALT II from Senate consideration, suspended shipments of grain and high-technology equipment to the Soviet Union, and initiated an international boycott of the 1980 Summer Olympics in Moscow. Although many American athletes voiced their support for the boycott, there were others, including Judy Napier, the wife of weightlifter Jim Napier, who were profoundly disappointed. Mrs. Napier

sent President Carter a telegram telling him he should reconsider his decision. In the end, the president refused to call off the boycott, but neither that nor any of his other actions against the Soviet Union brought about any changes in that country's policies.

NAPIER'S TELEGRAM TO PRESIDENT CARTER: 1980

… My husband has trained for 8 years … to make the U.S. Weight Lifting Team in Moscow. We have sacrificed our time, energy, personal income, and emotions to have this dream come true.… There are thousands of other athletes like him. Please reconsider your boycott. We are not politicians. The differences between countries should not be manifested in athletics. Our sacrifices have been many. We count too.

CARTER AND THE MIDDLE EAST

In 1973, Egypt led an unsuccessful Arab attack against Israel in what was called the Yom Kippur War. Two months after the attack, representa-

▲ President Sadat (*left*), President Carter (*center*), and Prime Minister Begin (*right*) shake hands after signing the peace treaty.

tives of Israel, Egypt, Syria, Jordan, the United States, and the Soviet Union met to discuss a permanent peace settlement for the Middle East, but no progress was made until November 19, 1977, when Egyptian president Anwar el-Sadat stunned the world by visiting Israel. In September 1978, President Carter met with Sadat and Israeli prime minister Menachem Begin in the United States to work out a permanent peace settlement between their two countries. Under the Camp David Accords, as the documents were known, Israel completely withdrew from the Sinai Peninsula and normal diplomatic relations were established between the two countries. This meant that for the first time in its history, Israel was formally at peace with an Arab nation.

THE CAMP DAVID ACCORDS: 1978

... The following matters are agreed between the parties: ... Egyptian sovereignty up to the internationally recognized border between Egypt and mandated Palestine; the withdrawal of Israeli armed forces from the Sinai; the use of airfields left by the Israelis near al-Arish, Rafah, Ras en-Naqb, and Sharm el-Sheikh for civilian purposes only, including possible commercial use ... the right of free passage by ships of Israel through the Gulf of Suez and the Canal ... the Strait of Tiran and Gulf of Aqaba ... to be open to all nations for ... navigation and overflight; the construction of a highway between the Sinai and Jordan near Eilat with guaranteed free and peaceful passage by Egypt and Jordan; ... the stationing of ... no more than one division (mechanized or infantry) of Egyptian armed forces ... within an area lying approximately [30 miles] east of the Gulf of Suez and the Suez Canal ... [and] ... Israeli ... military forces not to exceed four infantry battalions....

The formal peace treaty was signed in Washington on March 26, 1979. On October 6, 1981, while observing a military parade, President Sadat was assassinated by members of Al Jihad, a group of religious extremists opposed to recognition of Israel. The treaty still holds to this day.

▲ An American hostage is led around by his Iranian captors.

HOSTAGES IN IRAN

Carter's success with Egypt and Israel was offset by his failure in Iran, another Middle East hot spot. On November 4, 1979, militant Iranian students, opposed to their former ruler's being admitted to an American hospital for treatment of cancer, seized the American Embassy in Tehran and held fifty-two Americans hostage for more than a year under sometimes harsh and terrifying conditions. Robert C. Ode, a retired diplomat on special assignment to Tehran, was one of the Americans

ROBERT C. ODE'S DIARY: 1979–1981

September 26, 1980: I told [one of the Iranian students] that [he and the other students] were exceptionally cruel and unkind, which he denied, saying that they were not "terrorists" but students, but I told him that when I am kept ... in a locked room, constantly guarded ... with loaded guns, when I couldn't even go to the toilet ... without being blindfolded and constantly guarded— then, in my opinion, they were terrorists.... I reminded him again that ... the U.S. Government would never agree to negotiate with "gangsters and terrorists" and that while they may not consider themselves to be terrorists and gangsters, that is exactly what they are regarded in the eyes of the world.

taken hostage. He kept a diary during his captivity.

At first, President Carter tried negotiating for the release of the hostages through countries that still had diplomatic ties with Iran, but when that failed, he ordered a rescue mission, which also failed.

On January 19, 1981—Carter's last day in office—the United States and Iran, with help from Algeria, signed an accord on the release of the American hostages. Rather than release the hostages on that day, however, the hostages were released moments after Ronald Reagan had taken the presidential oath of office— a direct snub to President Carter.

CARTER'S REPORT ON THE FAILED RESCUE: 1980

… On April 24, 1980, elements of the United States Armed Forces under my direction commenced the positioning stage of a rescue … of the American hostages.…

Six U.S. … transport aircraft and eight … helicopters entered Iran airspace.… Crews were not equipped for combat.…

During the flight … two of the eight helicopters developed operating difficulties.… Of the six [remaining] helicopters, one developed a serious hydraulic problem … [and] … it was determined that the operation could not proceed as planned.…

During the process of withdrawal, one of the helicopters accidentily collided with one of the C-130 aircraft … resulting in the death of eight personnel and the injury of several others. At this point, the decision was made to load all surviving personnel aboard the remaining C-130 aircraft and to abandon the remaining helicopters at the landing site. No United States Armed Forces remain in Iran.…

The mission on which [the American forces] were embarked was a humanitarian mission. It was not directed against Iran. It was not directed against the people of Iran. It caused no Iranian casualties.…

"The mission on which [the American forces] were embarked was a humanitarian mission. "

17

CHAPTER 3

The Reagan Years

1980–1988

Although President Carter had withstood a challenge from Senator Edward Kennedy of Massachusetts to represent the Democratic party in the 1980 presidential election, he was clearly a weakened president because of the Iranian hostage crisis and his inability to turn the economy around. The Republican party had also gone through some primary battles, but it came out united after its convention, with a ticket made up of Ronald Reagan and George H. W. Bush. Reagan, a former Hollywood actor and governor of California, struck a chord with voters with his message of lower taxes, smaller government, and renewed American power. Reagan defeated Jimmy Carter by the huge electoral vote margin of 489 to 49.

ASSASSINATION ATTEMPT

In the late 1970s and early 1980s, John Hinckley Jr., a college dropout and former psychiatric patient, was obsessed with actress Jodie Foster. On March 30, 1981, Hinckley wrote Foster a letter, telling her that he was going to shoot President Reagan, who had been in office only a few weeks, in order to gain Foster's

▲ James Brady and a police officer lay wounded after John Hinckley Jr.'s attempt to assassinate President Reagan.

Dear Jodie,

There is a definite possibility that I will be killed in my attempt to get Reagan. It is for this very reason that I am writing you this letter now....

As you well know by now, I love you very much....

Jodie, I would abandon this idea of getting Reagan in a second if I could only win your heart and live out the rest of my life with you, whether it be in total obscurity or whatever.... By sacrificing my freedom and possibly my life I hope to change your mind about me. This letter is being written an hour before I leave for the Hilton Hotel.

Jodie, I'm asking you to please look into your heart and at least give me the chance with this historical deed to gain your respect and love.

I love you forever.

love and respect. After mailing the letter, Hinckley walked to the Hilton Hotel in Washington, D.C., where he stood with a crowd, waiting for Reagan to appear. When he saw the president, Hinckley started firing.

President Reagan was shot in the chest but recovered completely after surgery to remove the bullets. A Secret Service agent and a policeman were also wounded, and press secretary James Brady was shot in the head. At his trial on June 21, 1982, John Hinckley was found not guilty by reason of insanity. As a result of the assassination attempt, the Brady Bill was passed in 1993, requiring a short waiting period during which a background check would be conducted on the purchaser of a handgun.

REAGANOMICS

"Reaganomics" was the term used to describe President Reagan's plan to solve the economic problems of the United States by not only cutting personal income taxes but also cutting billions of dollars from welfare programs. Reagan believed that lower taxes for the rich would provide them with more money to invest in new businesses, which would create new jobs for more people, thus enabling prosperity to "trickle down" to the poor. In August 1981, Congress passed the Economic Recovery Tax

Act, which cut personal income taxes. Congress also cut more than $30 billion from such domestic programs as Medicare, Medicaid, food stamps, welfare subsidies, and school meals. As a result, poverty deepened for many of the already poor. Women and nonwhites were particularly hard hit, as they were usually the last hired and the first laid off. For many of the poorest families in New York City in the 1980s, shabby hotels run by welfare agencies were the only shelter available. Writer and social critic Jonathan Kozol described such a hotel in one of his books.

KOZOL'S *RACHEL AND HER CHILDREN:* 1988

66 Wanda's been here fifteen months, has four kids, no hot plate, and no food in the refrigerator. 99

... She takes me to her cousin Wanda's room. I measure it: nine feet by twelve, a little smaller than the room in which I store my files on the homeless. Wanda's been here fifteen months, has four kids, no hot plate, and no food in the refrigerator. She's had no food stamps and no restaurant allowance for two months. I ask why.... She's curled up in a tattered slip and a torn sweater on a mattress with no sheet. Her case was closed, she says. Faintly, I hear something about "an application." Her words are hard to understand. I ask her whether she was here for Christmas. The very few words she speaks come out in small reluctant phrases: "Where else would I go!" She says her children got some presents from the fire department. There's a painting of Jesus and Mary on the wall above the bed. "My mother gave it to me." ...

REAGAN AND THE SOVIET UNION

President Reagan firmly believed that the Soviet Union was intent on promoting Communist revolutions around the world. To deal with this threat, Reagan spent more than $100 billion during his first term in office to strengthen America's military position in the world, especially in Western Europe, further chilling relations between the United States and the Soviet Union. However, in 1985, during Reagan's second term, Mikhail Gorbachev came to power in the Soviet Union. He was a proponent of *glasnost* (openness) and *perestroika* (reform). Reagan and Gorbachev met in Geneva in 1985 and in Iceland a year later without reaching an agreement on any major issues.

▲ **President Reagan and Secretary General Gorbachev meet in Geneva, Switzerland, in 1985.**

On June 12, 1987, President Reagan gave a speech in West Berlin, but it was also heard in East Berlin (in Soviet-controlled East Germany), because the president was standing in front of the Brandenburg Gate— part of the Berlin Wall separating the two cities.

In December, the two leaders finally achieved a breakthrough on arms reduction during a summit in

REAGAN'S SPEECH AT THE BRANDENBURG GATE: 1987

▲ President Reagan delivers a speech at the Brandenburg Gate.

… We hear much from Moscow about a new policy of reform and openness….

There is one sign the Soviets can make that would be unmistakable, that would advance dramatically the cause of freedom and peace….

General Secretary Gorbachev, if you seek peace, if you seek prosperity for the Soviet Union and Eastern Europe, if you seek liberalization: Come here to this gate! Mr. Gorbachev, open this gate! Mr. Gorbachev, tear down this wall!…

Washington, D.C., where they signed the Intermediate-Range Nuclear Forces (INF) Treaty, agreeing to destroy more than twenty-five hundred nuclear missile warheads. Relations between the two countries improved almost immediately. President Reagan received a warm welcome when he visited Moscow in the spring of 1988. At that time, Premier Gorbachev announced the start of the withdrawal of Russian troops from Afghanistan.

THE CHALLENGER DISASTER

On January 28, 1986, the space shuttle *Challenger* took off from Cape Canaveral, Florida, with a crew of seven that included schoolteacher Christa McAuliffe. Seconds after liftoff, the shuttle exploded as millions of spectators and television viewers watched. Everyone on board was killed. In a speech to the nation, President Reagan said, "We will never forget them … as they … waved good bye and 'slipped the surly bonds of earth' to 'touch the face of God.'" NASA (the National Aviation and Space Administration) canceled all scheduled flights, while the entire space program was reviewed. Shuttle missions were resumed in September 1988.

IRAN-CONTRA AFFAIR

Although the president had promised on several occasions that he would never negotiate with terrorists, Americans learned in November 1986 that their government had sold antitank missiles to Iran to win the release of American hostages in Lebanon. The controversy widened when it was revealed that Marine Lieutenant Colonel Oliver North, a member of the National Security Council, had funneled profits from the Iranian arms sales to the Contras, who were rebel forces in Nicaragua. This was a clear violation of congressional legislation against providing aid to guerrilla armies in any country.

In 1987, a congressional committee held televised hearings to find out the truth of what became known as the "Iran-Contra Affair." The final

▲ President Reagan and First Lady Nancy Reagan at the *Challenger* memorial service in 1986.

report stopped just short of accusing President Reagan of committing a crime in office, but Colonel Oliver North was convicted of destroying and falsifying documents, taking public funds for personal use, and aiding the obstruction of the United States Congress.

FINAL REPORT OF THE INDEPENDENT COUNSEL FOR IRAN-CONTRA MATTERS: 1993

… The underlying facts of Iran/Contra are that, regardless of criminality, President Reagan, the Secretary of State, the Secretary of Defense, and the Director of Central Intelligence and their necessary assistants committed themselves, however reluctantly, to two programs contrary to congressional policy and contrary to national policy. They skirted the law, some of them broke the law, and almost all of them tried to cover up the President's willful activities.…

The Independent Counsel [Lawrence E. Walsh] believes that to the extent possible, the central Iran/Contra crimes were vigorously prosecuted and the significant acts of obstruction were fully charged.…

"They skirted the law, some of them broke the law, and almost all of them tried to cover up the President's willful activities."

THE STOCK MARKET CRASH OF 1987

During the 1980s, stock prices increased steadily, and people spent a lot of their savings and even borrowed money to buy as many shares as they could, but on October 19, 1987, the market crashed, bringing an end to the spending spree. President Reagan claimed that the American economy was still sound, but some economists were not convinced. They blamed the crash on problems created by Reaganomics, citing that imports far outnumbered exports and that the federal government and individual citizens were borrowing more money than they could ever repay. The country did enter a recession, but it wasn't plunged into a depression. The economy didn't really start to improve again until the mid-1990s.

CHAPTER 4

The First George Bush

1988–1992

Although Americans knew that President Reagan's successor would have to deal with the serious downturn in the economy, the presidential election of 1988 generated a very small voter turnout, and Vice President George H. W. Bush was elected over the Democratic candidate, Massachusetts governor Michael Dukakis.

President George H. W. Bush had been a former envoy to China, a United Nations ambassador, and the director of the CIA, so he was very comfortable dealing with foreign policy. He was not as comfortable with domestic issues, and these were what plagued his administration.

During his campaign, Bush promised not to raise taxes, and emphasized the point at the Republican convention by saying, "Read my lips: No new taxes." But faced with a national debt near $3 trillion and out-of-control government spending, he was forced to go back on that promise, and raised taxes.

In the 1980s, savings and loan institutions were allowed to compete with banks, but when their high-risk investments went bad, the S&Ls failed, and the government had to bail them out with taxpayers' money in order to prevent a major economic disaster.

▲ President George H. W. Bush takes the oath of office at his inauguration on January 20, 1989.

THE AIDS HEALTH THREAT

In 1981, a strange new disease called Acquired Immune Deficiency Syndrome (AIDS) started occurring in the United States. Scientists discovered it was caused by HIV—the human immunodeficiency virus—and the number of deaths from it grew at an alarming rate. Homosexual men were the first ones to get it, but doctors soon realized that the virus was transmitted by blood transfusions, shared drug needles, and heterosexual sex, and anyone could get it. In 1987, Surgeon General C. Everett Koop encouraged the use of condoms as one method of preventing HIV infection. He said, "AIDS kills—and sexually active people have to be told this."

By the year 2000, the American death toll from AIDS had reached almost half a million. Ed Wolf, a volunteer AIDS counselor, wrote about how the disease affected not only the dying but the living.

ED WOLF'S *A WEEK ON WARD 5A*: 1991

… Ann spoke to me this evening about her brother, who is dying of AIDS…. The doctors told her last week that Ken wouldn't live past Friday, and now, two days later, he's still alive. We spoke about the dying process and why it might be taking him so long to die. Is he ready yet? Has he said his goodbyes? Has she said hers?

She spoke tenderly, of how her brother's impending death has reopened for her an old wound, the death of her infant daughter several years ago.

We discuss … her ability to deal, and to cope, and to find a way to carry the immeasurable sadness she is experiencing….

Today is my last day on the ward before a three-day weekend … and I have made plans to go to the mountains….

When I get to the hospital I see that Ken is still alive…. I go and say goodbye to [him]…. Ken's breathing seems very faint, too delicate and weak to be keeping him alive. As I leave, I know I will not see him again….

> **"Ann spoke to me this evening about her brother, who is dying of AIDS."**

THE COLLAPSE OF THE SOVIET UNION

When Mikhail Gorbachev became premier of the Soviet Union in 1985, he introduced two reforms: greater freedom of the press and limited free enterprise. Individuals, instead of the government, were allowed to own some businesses and to express themselves more freely. People in the Communist countries of Eastern Europe wanted the same liberties.

In 1989, the people of Poland demanded that their Communist rulers leave office so that the Polish people could form a democratic government. The fall of Communist Poland was quickly followed by two other Communist countries, Czechoslovakia and Romania.

In November 1989, Germans tore down the Berlin Wall, which separated Communist East Berlin and the rest of East Germany from demo-cratic West Berlin. Within a year, the two Germanies were reunited under a single democratic government.

Late in 1991, the Soviet Union itself collapsed, when the Soviet congress, under the leadership of Mikhail Gorbachev, voted to dis-solve the Union of Soviet Socialist Republics (U.S.S.R.) and to form fifteen independent republics.

▲ Built in 1961, the Berlin Wall separated East and West Germany. It was torn down in 1989.

THE GULF WAR

On August 2, 1990, Saddam Hussein, the dictator of oil-rich Iraq, invaded and occupied neighboring Kuwait, using the excuse that the small nation was really Iraqi territory. The Bush administration organized a coalition of thirty-four countries to block trade with Iraq and to protect the vital oil supplies of the region.

At the end of November 1990, the United Nations approved the use of force to liberate Kuwait if Iraq had not withdrawn by January 15, 1991. In a letter to his family, written just before Christmas, President Bush talked about the difficult decisions he would be facing in the next few days.

PRESIDENT BUSH'S LETTER TO HIS CHILDREN: 1990

Dear George, Jeb, Neil, Marvin, Doro[thy],

… We are a family blessed; and this Christmas simply reinforced all that.… I have thought long and hard about what might have to be done [about Iraq's invasion of Kuwait].… We have gone to the U.N.; we have formed an historical coalition; there have been diplomatic initiatives from country after country.… We are 16 days from … the date set by the U.N. for his [Saddam Hussein] … getting out of Kuwait—totally.

I guess what I want you to know as a father is this:

Every human life is precious. When the question is asked "How many lives are you willing to sacrifice" … the answer, of course, is none—none at all. We have … moved a tremendous force so as to reduce the risk to every American soldier … but the question of loss of life still lingers and plagues the heart.…

Saddam cannot profit in any way at all from his aggression and from his brutalizing the people of Kuwait.…

And sometimes … you have to act as you think best—you can't compromise, you can't give in … even if your critics are loud and numerous.…

And so I shall say a few more prayers, mainly for our [military] kids in the Gulf, and I shall do what must be done.… I shall be strengthened … by our family love.… I am the luckiest Dad in the whole wide world.…

The Persian Gulf War, known officially as Operation Desert Storm, began on January 17, 1991, with a massive air campaign. The ground war began on February 24 and lasted only a few days. Kuwait was now free, but Saddam Hussein and his Republican Guards were left in power in Iraq, something that would come to haunt not only George H. W. Bush but also the next two presidents.

At home, President Bush's popularity soared after the war. Most Americans believed that he would win reelection in 1992, but as the economy continued to weaken, the president's approval ratings declined, and Bill Clinton, the Democratic candidate and former governor of Arkansas, won the election.

CHAPTER 5

The Clinton Years

1992–2000

Bill Clinton won the 1992 presidential election on a platform that focused largely on domestic issues. Shortly after taking office, Clinton fulfilled a campaign promise by signing the Family and Medical Leave Act. It required large employers to allow their employees to take unpaid leave because of a family or medical emergency.

Although this action was popular, another campaign promise—to force the military to accept homosexual

▲ President Bill Clinton and his wife, Hillary Rodham Clinton.

THE FAMILY AND MEDICAL LEAVE ACT: 1993

... The number of single-parent households and two-parent households in which the single parent or both parents work is increasing....

It is the purpose of this Act ... to balance the demands of the workplace with the needs of families, to promote the stability and economic security of families, and to promote national interests in preserving family integrity; to entitle employees to take reasonable leave for medical reasons, for the birth or adoption of a child, and for the care of a child, spouse, or parent who has a serious health condition; [and] to accomplish [this] in a manner that accommodates the legitimate interests of employers....

servicemen and service-women—was not. Eventually Clinton and the Pentagon (the Washington, D.C., headquarters of all military branches) agreed to a "Don't ask, don't tell" policy.

President Clinton put First Lady Hillary Rodham Clinton (who became a U.S. senator from New York in 2000) in charge of trying to find a way to reform the nation's health-care system, but the attempt was unsuccessful, because the proposal was considered too complicated and relied too heavily on federal government support.

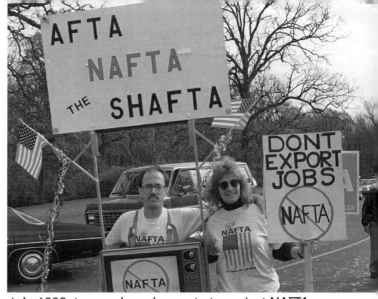

▲ In 1993, two workers demonstrate against NAFTA.

NAFTA

In the 1992 presidential election, one of the major issues was the North American Free Trade Agreement (NAFTA), which proposed establishing a free-trade zone for the United States, Canada, and Mexico. This meant that companies could buy and sell goods to each other as if they were operating in the same country. From the very beginning, controversy surrounded NAFTA.

Companies that were already doing business in Canada, Mexico, and the United States supported it, because they believed that no tariffs (taxes on imported goods) would lead to higher profits for them. Labor unions in the United States opposed NAFTA. They feared that jobs would move out of the country because of lower labor costs in Mexico. Mexican farmers opposed NAFTA because they knew that U.S. government subsidies to American farmers—which kept agricultural prices low—would force them to sell their products for less and probably put many of them out of business.

Environmental advocacy groups opposed NAFTA because they believed it would impact the environment in negative ways. They pointed to Mexico's less-strict pollution laws, charging that Mexican long-haul trucks would pollute the air. Still, most people believe that NAFTA has provided consumers with more choices of products at competitive prices.

The Contract with America

Tired of Democratic-controlled Congresses, Newt Gingrich, a Republican representative from Georgia, came up with a ten-point legislative agenda called the "Contract with America" during the 1994 mid-term elections. Through this legislation, Republican members of the House of Representative promised "to restore the bonds of trust between the people and their elected representatives" by reforming inefficient and wasteful government programs and procedures.

The contract was supported by Republican representatives and Republican candidates for Congress.

In the elections, the Republican party scored a stunning victory. It won both houses of Congress for the first time since 1954. Gingrich became speaker of the House, and Bob Dole of Kansas became majority leader of the Senate. Although many parts of the Contract were eventually enacted, others either didn't pass Congress or were vetoed by President Clinton.

The Contract with America: 1994

… The Contract with America is rooted in three core principles: accountability, responsibility, and opportunity.…

On the first day of the 104th Congress, the new Republican majority will immediately pass the following major reforms, aimed at restoring the faith and trust of the American people in their government:

… require all laws that apply to the rest of the country also apply equally to the Congress; … select a major, independent auditing firm to conduct a comprehensive audit of Congress for waste, fraud or abuse; … cut the number of House committees, and cut committee staff by one-third; … limit the terms of all committee chairs; … ban the casting of proxy votes in committee; … require committee meetings to be open to the public; … require a three-fifths majority vote to pass a tax increase; … guarantee an honest accounting of our Federal Budget by implementing zero base-line budgeting.…

Respecting the judgment of our fellow citizens as we seek their mandate for reform, we hereby pledge our names to this Contract with America.…

▲ The Alfred P. Murrah Federal Building after it was bombed by Timothy McVeigh.

OKLAHOMA CITY BOMBING

On April 19, 1995, Timothy McVeigh, a 26-year-old Gulf War veteran, detonated a truck full of explosives in front of the Alfred P. Murrah Federal Building in downtown Oklahoma City, killing one hundred sixty-eight people. McVeigh thought that the federal government was abusing its power, and he hoped that the Oklahoma City bombing would cause other militants across the nation to take similar action.

McVeigh and Terry Nichols, a co-conspirator, were soon caught, tried, and found guilty. Nichols was sentenced to life in prison. McVeigh was sentenced to death and was executed at the state penitentiary in McAlester, Oklahoma, in 2001.

DOMESTIC POLICIES

In August 1996, President Clinton signed legislation that marked a major change in welfare policy. He wanted to decrease spending on unemployed citizens and encourage them to find jobs.

Despite friction between President Clinton and Congress, the U.S. economy experienced one of its longest periods of uninterrupted growth in history. When Congress approved Clinton's plan for reducing the federal budget deficit, the economy improved even more, and the president was able to take credit for it.

President Clinton won reelection in 1996 over the Republican candidate, Senator Bob Dole of Kansas.

VIOLENCE IN YUGOSLAVIA

In the 1990s, Slobodan Milosevic, who was the president of Yugoslavia as well as the leader of Serbia—the largest province in Yugoslavia—sent his army into the provinces of Croatia and Bosnia, which were trying to secede from the country. After centuries of hatred and wars, Milosevic wanted to "ethnically cleanse" the two provinces—that is, kill all the Croats and Bosnians. The rest of the world looked to the United States—now the only true superpower—to stop these "crimes against humanity."

With the help of its NATO allies, the United States did what it could militarily to bring about an end to the centuries-old blood feuds of the Balkans. At meetings in Dayton, Ohio, in 1995, President Clinton helped Bosnia and Croatia sign a truce with Serbia. He hoped this would end the violence in the region, but when Milosevic intensified his campaign against ethnic Albanians in the break-away province of Kosovo in March 1999, NATO bombed military targets there and in the rest of Serbia. Milosevic withdrew his forces in June, and a multinational force under the United Nations was sent to keep the peace.

DAYTON [OHIO] ACCORDS: 1995

... The Republic of Bosnia and Herzegovina, the Republic of Croatia, and the Federal Republic of Yugoslavia [Serbia] ... [recognize] the need ... to bring an end to the tragic conflict in the region....

[They agree to] ... the principles set forth in the United Nations Charter ... [and] shall fully respect the sovereign equality of one another, shall settle disputes by peaceful means, and shall refrain from any action, by threat or use of force ... against the territorial integrity or political independence of Bosnia and Herzegovina or any other State....

Basic human rights, in particular freedom of movement, freedom of association, and the right of resettlement must be honored fully.

◀ A cartoon depicts Slobodan Milosevic standing among slaughtered Bosnians.

CLINTON SCANDALS

Even before the 1992 presidential election, scandals threatened to end Clinton's campaign. He admitted that he had been unfaithful to his wife, but the voters elected him for what they thought he could do for the country as president.

In 1994, President and Mrs. Clinton were accused of unethical practices in a failed real estate development called Whitewater, but after a six-year investigation by independent counsel Kenneth Starr, there was insufficient evidence to bring criminal charges against them.

Before the 1996 presidential elec-

▲ President Clinton and Monica Lewinsky greet each other at a public gathering.

tion, several women accused President Clinton of sexual harassment when he was governor of Arkansas, charges he denied, but he was reelected for a second term anyway.

In 1998 the president was accused of having an affair with a young White House intern, Monica Lewinsky, who, in 1997 sent him a short note, lamenting how difficult it was to be away from him. Clinton finally admitted to his inappropriate behavior, but because he had denied the relationship in a sworn statement, it now appeared that he had committed perjury, or lied to the court. For this serious offense, the House of Representatives voted to impeach the president, but on February 12, 1999, the Senate voted to acquit him.

LEWINSKY'S LETTER TO PRESIDENT CLINTON: 1997

Handsome:

I asked you ... to please be sensitive to what I am going through right now and to keep in contact with me, and yet I'm still left writing notes in vain.... When I saw you ... in August ... you were so distant....

I am begging you to please be nice to me.... I need you right now....

CHAPTER 6

The Second George Bush

2000–2004

As the United States entered a new century and a new millennium, Americans were faced with a controversial presidential election. On election night, November 7, 2000, the Florida vote count, which would determine the new president, was still in doubt. Subsequent recount estimates showed that Bush had won by a few hundred votes, and after more recounts and numerous court appeals on both sides—including one to the U.S. Supreme Court—George W. Bush, the son of former president George H. W. Bush, was declared the winner. Although in the end, Vice President Al Gore had more individual votes throughout the country, Bush had more Electoral College votes, and this was the determining factor in who would be president.

Once in office, President Bush put aside the election controversy and pushed for the passage of his Economic Growth and Tax Reform Reconciliation Act, which he hoped would stimulate the economy by

---

"... lower income taxes for all, with the greatest help for those more in need."

BUSH'S REMARKS ON HIS 2001 TAX CUT PROPOSAL: 2001

... These are the basic ideas that guide my tax policy: lower income taxes for all, with the greatest help for those more in need. Everyone who pays income taxes benefits—while the highest percentage tax cuts go to the lowest income Americans.... It is an economics of inclusion.... A tax plan must apply market principles to the public interest.... My plan sets out to make life better for average men, women, and children....

giving people more money to spend. Opponents alleged that his tax cut proposal favored the wealthy, but both houses of Congress passed a modified version, and the president signed it into law.

BUSH'S FOREIGN POLICY

President Bush made it clear from the beginning of his administration that he planned to pursue a unilateral (go it alone) approach to American foreign policy. Right away, he disengaged from the Kyoto global warming accord, because he thought it would hurt American companies, and abolished the 1972 Anti-Ballistic Missile Treaty with Russia because he believed it would hinder the nation's ability to fight terrorism.

On April 1, 2001, a navy surveillance plane reported that it had been hit by a Chinese fighter plane that was closely tailing it off the China coast. The Chinese plane crashed into the South China Sea. The damaged U.S. plane, with twenty-four crew members and secret equipment, made an emergency landing on the Chinese island of Hainan. The Chinese government accused the U.S. aircraft of ramming the jet fighter, and they wanted an apology from Washington before they would release the crew. The wife of the Chinese

RUAN GUOQIN'S LETTER TO PRESIDENT BUSH: 2001

...What is incredible is you and your government's apathetic attitude toward my husband's life.... With irrefutable facts and the responsibility completely resting on the U.S. side, you are too cowardly to voice an apology and have ... defamed my husband groundlessly. Can this be the human rights and humanism that you have been talking about?... [My husband's jet was] rammed by a spy plane of your country.... I grieve for the loss of my beloved husband.... Give me a reason! Bring back my husband!...

pilot who died, Ruan Guoqin, also wrote an angry letter to President Bush. A week later, the U.S. government issued a formal statement that it regretted the incident.

China announced on April 11 that it was releasing all the crew members but not the plane itself. Once they were back in the United States, the crew confirmed that the plane's secret equipment had been destroyed before the Chinese authorities boarded it, and as far as the United States was concerned, the matter was closed.

THE 9/11 ATTACKS

On September 11, 2001, four passenger planes were hijacked by members of an Islamist terrorist organization called al-Qaida. Two of the planes were flown directly into the twin towers of the World Trade Center in New York City, causing the towers to come crashing down. One of the hijacked planes was flown into the Pentagon in Washington, D.C., causing immense damage and loss of life. The fourth hijacked plane crashed in a field in Pennsylvania, when passengers rushed the hijackers. On September 11, 2004, the *Washington Post* reported that the death toll was 2,749 in the World Trade Center towers, 184 in the Pentagon, and 264 in the four airliners (including the hijackers).

Messages of sympathy from all over the world flooded the country. When President Bush started to speak to rescue workers at "ground zero," where the twin towers had stood, a fireman shouted, "I can't hear you!" The president responded, "I can hear you. The rest of the world hears you. And the people who knocked down these buildings will hear all of us soon. Thank you for your hard work. Thank you for making the nation proud, and may God bless America."

▲ The twin towers of the World Trade Center are on fire after two hijacked planes crashed into them.

INTERNATIONAL RESPONSES TO THE 9/11 ATTACKS: 2001

▲ President Bush comforts N.Y. firefighters after the 9/11 attacks.

United Nations Security Council Resolution 1368, September 12:
… The Security Council … condemns in the strongest terms the horrifying terrorist attacks which took place on 11 September 2001 … and regards such acts, like any act of international terrorism, as a threat to international peace and security; expresses its deepest sympathy and condolences to the victims and their families and to the People and Government of the United States.…

Statement from British prime minister Tony Blair:
… The full horror of what has happened in the United States earlier today is now becoming clearer.… We've offered President Bush and the American people our solidarity, our profound sympathy, and our prayers.… Flight paths into London have been changed.… Security has been increased across the full range of government buildings and military premises. The police across the whole of the [United Kingdom] are on full alert.…

Statement from Judy Sgro, member of Canadian Parliament:
… Death and destruction are never pleasant, but what happened [on September 11] was extraordinarily disgusting. Wanton killing, the murder of innocent people, destruction of property and terrorism have no place in the civilized society we all cherish in [Canada].

… Canada is a democracy.… It opens its doors to offer hope and opportunity to everyone. However our values and hospitality must not be abused, and they have been. As a result Canada, along with the United States and free people everywhere, has been cast into a worldwide struggle against the forces of darkness.… There can be no alternative but absolute victory.…

THE WAR AGAINST TERRORISM

On October 8, the United States led a massive campaign of air strikes against Afghanistan to defeat the Taliban regime, to disrupt the al-Qaida terrorist network, and to find Osama Bin Laden, the Saudi-born terrorist who masterminded the September 11 attacks. But Bin Laden managed to evade U.S. capture.

Later that month, the U.S. Senate approved the Uniting and Strengthening America by Providing Appropriate Tools Required to Intercept and Obstruct Terrorism Act. Better known as the "Patriot Act," this controversial law gave the government, and especially the attorney general, permission to covertly investigate individuals suspected of being a threat to national security. There has been strong criticism of the Patriot Act by such groups as the American Civil Liberties Union, which believes that parts of the act violate the Constitution.

President Bush also signed into law in 2002 a bill creating a Department of Homeland Security—the biggest reorganization of the federal government in more than fifty years. The new department

▲ Osama Bin Laden, the mastermind behind the 9/11 attacks.

U.S. PATRIOT ACT: 2001

... Allows a wiretap to be granted against an individual, instead of a particular phone.

... Allows FBI agents to conduct a search of a business or a place without notifying the owner....

Allows law-enforcement ... to get a warrant to track which websites a person visits and collect general information about the emails a person sends and receives.

... Directs the Attorney General to implement fully and expand the foreign student monitoring program...

consolidated more than forty existing federal agencies—such as the U.S. Border Patrol, the U.S. Customs Services, and the Nuclear Incident Response Team—into a single cabinet agency. The purpose of this agency is to prevent terrorist attacks, reduce America's vulnerability to terrorism, and

manage the aftermath of any attack. Tom Ridge, the former governor of Pennsylvania, was chosen to head the new department.

President Bush speaks at a ceremony that marks the first official day of the Department of Homeland Security. ▶

BUSH'S REMARKS ON THE HOMELAND SECURITY ACT: 2002

… The new department will analyze threats, will guard our borders and airports, protect our critical infrastructure, and coordinate the response of our nation for future emergencies. [It] … will focus the full resources of the American government on the safety of the American people. This essential reform was carefully considered by Congress and enacted with strong bipartisan majorities.…

With … [this act] … we're doing everything we can to protect America. We're showing the resolve of this great nation to defend our freedom, our security, and our way of life.…

❝It … will focus the full resources of the American government on the safety of the American people.❞

FINANCIAL SCANDALS

In 2002, Enron, an energy trading and communications corporation based in Texas, was investigated by the U.S. Department of Justice for bribery and use of political pressure to secure contracts around the world. Enron went bankrupt, and several top executives were indicted. In the wake of the scandal, many Enron employees lost not only their jobs but most of their life savings as well.

The Enron affair was the first of a wave of accounting scandals involving big businesses. In light of the collapse of Enron, Representative John Boehner of Ohio gave a speech before the International Foundation of Employee Benefit Plans in which he advocated legislative action to protect workers against the "next Enron."

> **66** The Enron bankruptcy … left many loyal Enron workers with no retirement security at all. **99**

BOEHNER'S SPEECH BEFORE THE INTERNATIONAL FOUNDATION OF EMPLOYEE BENEFIT PLANS: 2002

… The Enron bankruptcy resulted in devastating losses to the company's employee 401(k) plan and left many loyal Enron workers with no retirement security at all.…

In early April … my own committee [House Education & the Workforce] … passed the Pension Security Act … that could have made a real difference for Enron's workers.…

The House [of Representatives] has taken [this] action to protect American workers against the "next Enron." President Bush is eager to sign this legislation into law. But instead of going to the White House [for] the President's signature, it's sitting over in the Senate gathering dust.…

WAR WITH IRAQ

In his January 28, 2003, State of the Union address to Congress, President Bush prepared Americans for a war with Iraq by detailing how Saddam Hussein was continuing to show his contempt for the United Nations and for the opinions of the world by refusing to allow U.N. weapons inspectors

TONY BLAIR'S SPEECH ON THE INVASION OF IRAQ: 2003

… On Tuesday night I gave the order for British forces to take part in military action in Iraq.…

The threat to Britain today is not that of my father's generation.… Europe is at peace. The Cold War is already a memory.…

But this new world faces a new threat: of disorder and chaos born either of brutal states like Iraq, armed with weapons of mass destruction; or of extreme terrorist groups. Both hate our way of life, our freedom, our democracy.…

So our choice is clear: back down and leave Saddam hugely strengthened; or proceed to disarm him by force. Retreat might give us a moment of respite but years of repentance at our weakness would I believe follow.…

to verify that he was getting rid of his weapons of mass destruction. With the support of British prime minister Tony Blair and a handful of world leaders, Bush proceeded with his plans for war with Iraq. On March 20, 2003, United States missile attacks on targets in Baghdad marked the start of the U.S.-led campaign to topple the Iraqi dictatorship. Prime Minister Tony Blair gave a televised address to his nation about the invasion of Iraq.

By early April, American forces had advanced into central Baghdad. Almost immediately guerrilla warfare broke out. The guerrillas used mortars, suicide bombers, roadside bombs, and small arms fire against the coali-tion forces—killing more than one thousand—as well as against Iraqi citizens who supported them. The guerrilla groups were organized by Saddam Hussein loyalists, religious radicals, Iraqis angered by the occupation, and foreign fighters.

▲ U.S. soldiers fighting in Iraq.

HUSSEIN AND WEAPONS OF MASS DESTRUCTION

Eight months after Baghdad fell, American soldiers found Saddam Hussein hiding in a six-foot-deep hole equipped with a basic ventilation system and covered with bricks and dirt. The location was about ten miles from Hussein's hometown of Tikrit. He had a pistol, but he was taken into custody without firing it. As word of Hussein's capture spread, crowds of Iraqis began celebrating in the streets. At his arraignment, Hussein insisted that he was still the rightful ruler of Iraq. Afterward, he was taken to Camp Cropper, near Baghdad International Airport, where he is expected to stay until he is put on trail by the new Iraqi government.

Although one of the justifications for going to war with Iraq was

Hussein's alleged arsenal of weapons of mass destruction (WMD), none were found. In February 2004, President Bush ordered an inquiry into pre-war intelligence on Iraq's WMD, which still had not been found. CIA director George Tenet defended the U.S. intelligence estimate of Iraq's suspected weapons program, but many Americans, including members of Congress, had no confidence in Tenet's explanation, and he later resigned as director.

THE NEW IRAQI GOVERNMENT

Iraq's interim government was sworn in on Monday, June 28, 2004, two days ahead of schedule. The official handover of sovereignty occurred when coalition civil administrator L. Paul Bremer gave interim prime minister Ayad Allawi a leather-bound transfer document. Some Iraqis dismissed the handover as meaningless as long as U.S. troops continued to occupy the nation, but others said the handover was a step in the right direction. President Bush said that the handover began a new phase in Iraq's progress toward full democracy, but he also announced that American troops would stay as long as the stability of Iraq required them.

Saddam Hussein after his capture in Iraq. ▶

THE 9/11 COMMISSION REPORT

In late 2002, the National Commission on Terrorist Attacks upon the United States (known as the 9/11 Commission) began investigating the events of September 11, 2001. The commission, independent of the government and made up of both Democrats and Republicans, issued its report in July 2004. The report provided a full account of the circumstances surrounding the terrorist attacks and concluded that the pre-9/11 intelligence could have been better. The report also included recommendations for guarding against future attacks.

THE 2004 PRESIDENTIAL ELECTION

During the 2004 presidential election, President Bush ran for a second term in office along with his vice president, Dick Cheney. Senators John Kerry of Massachusetts and John Edwards of North Carolina were the Democratic presidential and vice presidential candidates, respectively.

Much of the campaign was based on negative ads that focused on the perceived weaknesses of the other party's candidates. In the end, President Bush was reelected by a margin of twenty-two electoral votes and more than three million popular votes.

9/11 COMMISSION REPORT: 2004

The United States has the resources and the people. The government should combine them more effectively, achieving unity of effort. We offer … major recommendations to do that:

… [Unify] strategic intelligence and operation planning.…

[Unify] the intelligence community with a new National Intelligence Director;

… [Unify] the many participants in the counter-terrorism effort and their knowledge in a network-based information-sharing system that transcends traditional governmental boundaries;

… [Strengthen] the FBI and homeland defenders.…

❝The United States has the resources and the people.❞

TIME LINE

1970	■ Four Kent State University students are killed during an antiwar protest.
1972	■ President Nixon makes a historic visit to Communist China.
1972–1974	■ The Watergate scandal leads to President Nixon's resignation; Vice-President Gerald Ford becomes the thirty-eighth U.S. president.
1973	■ *Roe* v. *Wade*, a landmark Supreme Court case, legalizes abortion.
1973	■ The last United States troops leave Vietnam.
1975	■ The South Vietnamese government surrenders to North Vietnam.
1976	■ Jimmy Carter is elected the thirty-ninth U.S. president.
1979	■ Egypt and Israel sign the Camp David Accords, ending years of conflict.
1979–1981	■ Iranian students hold Americans hostage in Tehran.
1980	■ Ronald Reagan is elected the fortieth U.S. president.
1986	■ The space shuttle *Challenger* explodes, killing all crew members.
1987	■ President Reagan and Premier Gorbachev sign the INF treaty to reduce nuclear weapons.
1988	■ George H. W. Bush is elected the forty-first U.S. president.
1990–1991	■ The United States and its allies fight the Persian Gulf War.
1992	■ President Bush and Russian president Yeltsin declare an end to the Cold War.
1992	■ Bill Clinton is elected the forty-second U.S. president.
2000	■ George W. Bush is elected the forty-third U.S. president.
2001	■ Al-Qaida launches terrorist attacks on the United States.
2001	■ The United States and its allies attack the Taliban in Afghanistan.
2003	■ The U.S. and its allies invade Iraq; Saddam Hussein is captured.
2004	■ Iraq's interim government is sworn in, but the war continues.
2004	■ George W. Bush is elected for a second term as president.

GLOSSARY

abortion: termination of a pregnancy.

accord: agreement by nations to settle their differences.

AIDS: disease that attacks the body's immune system.

al-Qaida: Arabic Islamic terrorist organization.

Berlin Wall: concrete wall that surrounded West Berlin during the Cold War.

coalition: temporary alliance of nations.

condoms: rubber sheaths worn by males to prevent pregnancy or disease.

Contras: rebels fighting the government of Nicaragua.

détente: the easing of tensions between nations.

draft: military selection process.

food stamps: government-issued coupons for low-income families to purchase food.

401(k) plan: a type of retirement savings program.

glasnost: Russian for "openness."

health-care system: private and government-funded insurance and medical services that are available in the U.S.

human rights: what is fair and just for all people.

humanitarian: helping and promoting the well being of people.

inflation: abnormal increase in prices.

Medicaid: government program of medical care for the poor.

Medicare: government program of medical care for the elderly.

NAFTA: trade agreement among Canada, the United States, and Mexico.

National Guard: military units controlled by each state.

OPEC: international organization of oil-producing nations.

perestroika: Russian word for "reform."

post-traumatic stress disorder: psychological problems often caused by fighting in a war.

Reaganomics: economic policies of Ronald Reagan.

refugees: persons who flee from his or her country.

SALT: treaty that limited American and Soviet missiles.

sexual harassment: unwanted sexual attention from another person.

silent majority: Americans who agree with government policies but don't make their opinions known.

Taliban: government of Afghanistan that harbored terrorists.

Vietnamization: President Nixon's plan to return the fighting in Vietnam gradually back to the South Vietnamese.

welfare: economic and social aid to poor people.

FURTHER INFORMATION

BOOKS

Levy, Paricia. *The Fall of the Berlin Wall, November 9, 1989*, Days That Shook the World. Raintree Publishers, 2002.

Thoms, Annie. *With Their Eyes: September 11th—The View from a High School at Ground Zero.* HarperTempest, 2002.

Warren, Andrea. *Escape from Saigon: How a Vietnam War Orphan Became an American Boy.* Farrar, Straus and Giroux, 2004.

WEB SITES

www.911digitalarchive.org This Web site presents a digital history of the September 11 attacks through digital images, moving images, documents, and more. The site is associated with the Library of Congress and the American Red Cross.

www.vietvet.org This Web site was developed to honor Vietnam veterans. It contains stories, poems, songs, pictures and more that were written by Vietnam vets.

USEFUL ADDRESS

Vietnam Veterans Memorial
900 Ohio Drive, SW
Washington, DC 20024
Telephone: (202) 426-6841

★★★ INDEX ★★★

Middlebury Community Library